A Snowstorm
in Mississippi

Reflections of a Life Complete
Yet Unfinished

Janice Ann Slack

For permission requests, contact:

Know Wonder Publishing
Indianapolis, Indiana, USA
manager@dslack.com

ISBN 979-8-9921725-2-2

Cover Design: Anze Ban Virant
Edited by Know Wonder Publishing

Printed in the United States of America

This is a work of nonfiction. The events and reflections within are drawn from the author's personal experiences. Any fictionalized elements or composite characters are used solely to protect privacy and convey emotional truth.

Know Wonder Publishing ™

DEDICATION

To my children and grandchildren—
the roots and branches of my life.
May your days be guided by faith,
your hearts anchored in love,
and your steps forever grounded
in the legacy we began together.

— Grandma

TABLE OF CONTENTS

Chapter 1 | The Storm

They say that night, that strange, awful, beautiful night, the world itself was shifting. The cold rolled down from the mountains like a great, invisible river, chasing the warm, clear air right out of the Mississippi South. Folks in Oxford had never seen anything like it — the kind of cold that bites through your coat and settles into your bones. The kind of cold that makes you shiver, a twitch and tingle you get down your spine the way the old folks say means a rabbit is passing by your grave. My Mama said the sky turned the color of tin, and the earth went still, like it was waiting for something to happen.

That *something* wasn't just a storm, although there was a storm the likes of which people would talk about for generations — the Great Appalachian Storm of 1950. And it wasn't just a Mississippi storm either; it was a storm that swallowed half the country. From the hills of West Virginia to the fields of Tennessee, snow fell so thick it buried fences and silenced towns, even colder than they were at sundown.

In Ohio and West Virginia, folks woke up to more than two feet of snow, doors frozen shut, roads gone, roofs creaking under the weight. Along the East Coast, winds howled like angry spirits — fierce enough to snatch shingles off houses and bend trees in half. And while the North battled blizzards, the South froze. Still like a deer caught by the lights of an approaching vehicle. Temperatures dropped lower than anyone could remember. Water buckets turned solid, pipes burst, and the ponds froze so thick the children could walk across them.

In Tennessee and North Carolina, the cold broke records that still stand, so at least in those parts, it has never been colder in my lifetime. It surely must have been the kind of cold that made you thank God for every stick of firewood. Yet, not far away, on the storm's northern edge, people were walking in their short sleeves beneath strangely mild skies. It was as if the earth itself couldn't decide between winter and spring.

Meteorologists would later call it one of the most powerful and unusual storms of the 20th century. The Great Appalachian Storm began just before Thanksgiving in November 1950, stretching across 22 states from the Deep South to New England. It spun with the force of a winter hurricane. It was a collision of warm Atlantic air and cold Arctic winds that reshaped weather history.

More than 350 people lost their lives, and entire towns were buried in snow. Wind speeds reached 100 miles per hour along the coast, and barometers dropped so low that the system was later classified as a "meteorological superstorm." In Mississippi, the storm arrived not with blizzards, but with the sharp, unrelenting cold that froze the soil and stilled the air — a cold so deep it felt like the world was holding its breath. Holding its breath as if waiting for something to happen.

And that something wasn't only the beginning of a storm. It was the beginning of a life. Because right in the middle of all that confusion — snow swirling, winds howling, the heavens and earth in argument — I came into this world. It was November 26, 1950. It was a Sunday. I was born on the day named after what could not be seen: the sun. What a day I picked to escape the warmth of my Mama's womb.

I came into the world at home, wrapped not in hospital blankets but in quilts sewn by women who had lived through wars, segregation, and sorrow. And maybe that's why I've always felt like I was born into both struggle and strength. The world didn't stop for my birth, but it did freeze, slow it down a bit so that I can announce my arrival. And in that little wooden house on the edge of Oxford, life began for me in the middle of a storm — and storms would follow me, shaping me, reminding me what survival looks like. Mama said the midwife almost didn't make it through the storm. The roads were slick, and the snow kept falling, thick and steady, like heaven wouldn't stop until I cried my first cry.

They said I was born in a miracle, a storm baby, the kind of birth that makes people nod and whisper, *"She came here strong. The world had to fight to bring her in."* And maybe that's why, all my days, I've carried both the quiet of snow and the strength of wind inside me.

That's how my story began: during a snowstorm in Mississippi, in a house with a tin roof, under a sky gone white, on a night when everything froze solid. Everything but the woodburning stove in the corner. Everything but the warmth of Mama's breast against my brown skin. Everything but my heart, beating like a beacon calling to my future children and grandchildren, signaling to them, "I will find you. I will love you. And my love will keep you warm, even through any storm you may face in your life."

That storm didn't just mark my beginning — it *defined* it. Because from the start, life wanted me to know even in the fiercest cold, something beautiful, warm, and loving can be born.

Chapter 2 | Intention

I have always wanted to write a book. Words have followed me my whole life — in letters, in prayers, in the quiet things I never said out loud. But I never truly had the desire to write one about *my* life. Not because I thought my story wasn't worth telling, but because to write it down means to relive it — the joy and the pain, the laughter and the loss. Some memories sit softly on your heart; others are sharp enough to draw blood even after all these years.

Still, something in me began to stir — a whisper that grew louder with time. My children and grandchildren started asking questions, wanting to know not just *what happened*, but *who I was* before them. And the more I thought about it, the more I realized: if I didn't tell my story, someone else might try to, and they'd never tell it quite right.

So, I began to write and tell aloud my story— not to glorify my past, but to preserve it. I wanted my family to understand where they come from, to trace their roots back through red clay and rainstorms, laughter and struggle. I wanted them to see that who they are did not begin with them. It began with a line of women and men who loved hard, worked harder, and prayed even when their voices shook.

I want them to love every part of their unique journey — the beautiful, the broken, the becoming — because who we are isn't just a collection of seconds that turn into years. We are not simply our names, our jobs, or our flesh and blood.

Who we are is found in the way we love — in the hands we hold, the promises we keep, the prayers we whisper when no one else is listening. We are the sum of every laugh that healed us, every loss that changed us, and every moment that taught us grace.

We are the *aggregate of our experiences* — the unforgettable ones that still make us smile, and the ones we swore we'd never revisit but can't seem to forget. And somewhere in the middle of all that living, we discover that our stories are not just ours to keep.

They are *gifts* we leave behind — small pieces of our hearts, pressed between pages, waiting for someone we love to find them and say,

"Now I understand where I come from."

Chapter 3 | Mama's Voice

Mama didn't need to raise her hand to make a point. Her voice alone could still the room. It was a sound that carried authority — strong enough to hush a house full of children, yet soft enough to comfort a broken heart. When she called your name, it wasn't just sound; it was a command wrapped in love, a reminder that somebody cared enough to correct you.

Her name was Eloise Liggins Brown, born sometime between 1919 and 1921 in Oxford, Mississippi, but the official record has her being born Wednesday, March 2, 1921. She was the eleventh of twelve or thirteen children of Anna and Green Liggins. She was the granddaughter of Mollie and Peter Liggins. Half of her siblings never made it past infancy; their names lost to time, whispered only in family stories and churchyard graves. Back then, a baby's survival wasn't promised, especially if some of them were of questionable origin (she worked a lot at the Master's house). Each new cry in the night was a small miracle. Mama used to say, *"The Lord kept me here for a reason."*

She grew up fast, because the world didn't give her the luxury of childhood. Her Mama — my Grandma Anna — worked long days at the master's house, cooking, cleaning, scrubbing floors, and raising white folks' children while her own learned to fend for themselves. Grandma would hide bits of leftover food behind the stove, wrap them in cloth, and carry them home after sundown — just enough to stretch a meal and keep her family alive.

That kind of life leaves its mark. Mama learned early that the world wasn't built for Black women to rest. So she learned to stand tall instead. She learned to walk with purpose, to keep her back straight even when her heart was heavy. She learned that you didn't always have to fight with your hands — sometimes your dignity was the loudest resistance you could offer.

She was the kind of woman who taught lessons without ever opening a book. *"Do right, baby,"* she'd tell me, *"and right will follow you."*

I didn't understand it then. I thought doing right was about rules, manners. I thought maybe it was about staying out of trouble, finishing my chores, saying "yes ma'am" and "no sir." For some reason Mama would not allow us to say "yes ma'am" to her, she believed it was an artificial way to show respect to unrespectable white folks. And as I grew older, I realized what she really meant: that integrity outlasts everything — money, beauty, even luck. When you do right, you sleep better. When you do right, you walk freer.

When Mama spoke, you didn't interrupt. You didn't talk back. If she had to call your name twice, you were already in trouble — and you knew it. But she didn't believe in breaking a child's spirit. Her power wasn't in punishment. Her power was in presence.

She could turn a room quiet with a look. She could make you feel safe with a word. She could pray storms into silence. Like the one she quieted the day I was born.

After a meal, Mama would tell stories — ghost stories, funny stories, and the kind that carried lessons tucked between the laughter. I can still hear her voice even now, deep and full, wrapping around the room like warm smoke from the wood-burning stove. Mama didn't own much, but she owned herself — her time, her tone, her truth. And that, more than anything, made her rich.

Women in my mother's time carried the world on their backs and were expected to do it quietly. In the early twentieth century, women — especially Black women in the South — had few rights and even fewer choices. They could not vote, could not own property freely, and were rarely allowed to dream beyond their kitchen walls. Their worth was often measured in how well they could keep house, raise children, and hold a man's world together without complaint.

Yet, in the shadow of those limits, women like my Mama built their own kind of power. They learned how to survive systems that weren't made for them, and how to outthink men who underestimated them. They made a dollar stretch like a mile, fed a family from a garden, and kept a roof over their heads with prayer and grit.

My mother, Eloise, understood that the world didn't see women like her as equals — so she made herself undeniable. She believed in the kind of education you couldn't take away. She could read and write when many others could not, and she made sure we understood that literacy was liberation. "If you can read, baby," I can feel her say, "then you can think for yourself."

Education, to her, wasn't about schooling, per se, it was about survival. It meant being able to sign your name instead of leaving an X on a paper you didn't understand. It meant counting your own money, reading a bill before you paid it, knowing what the preacher said for yourself instead of taking someone else's word for it.

And though women weren't welcome in banks, boardrooms, or politics, my Mama knew how to handle money better than most men. She could make ten dollars behave like a hundred. She saved coins in jars, folded bills in her Bible, and somehow always had enough to feed us, clothe us, and help a neighbor in need.

She may not have had the right to vote, but she had a voice — and she used it. She didn't march on Washington or speak from podiums, but every meal she cooked, every child she raised, every lesson she taught was a quiet act of resistance.

Women like her didn't just endure history — they shaped it, one humble miracle at a time.

Chapter 4 | Diddy's Hands

His hands told the story before his mouth ever could. Large, broad, and rough as the land itself, they were the first thing people noticed about him — those deep, almond-colored hands that looked like they'd been carved from Mississippi soil. The skin was thick and calloused, the color of roasted coffee, worn smooth in places by decades of work. The lines on his palms ran deep, like the furrows he once cut into the fields, and no matter how much lye soap or scrubbing he did, the stains of labor and tobacco never left.

Those hands had known every kind of work a man could do — chopping wood before dawn, laying fence posts in the summer heat, picking cotton until his fingers bled, mending plows with little more than wire and willpower. His knuckles were swollen from years of gripping tools too tightly, and faint scars traced the stories of accidents he never complained about — a hammer slip here, a splinter there, a nail that missed its mark.

There was strength in those hands, yes, the kind that could lift a full sack of cotton onto a wagon without strain, but there was gentleness, too. When he held a child, he made sure his rough palms never scraped soft skin. When he prayed, he folded those same scarred fingers together with reverence, the dirt of the day still beneath his nails but the purity of faith shining through.

In winter, his knuckles cracked and bled, but he kept on working. In summer, sweat ran down his forearms, stinging the open cuts that never had time to heal. He wrapped them in rags, tied them tight, and carried on. There was no such thing as rest for a Black man in Mississippi born in 1908 — not if he wanted to feed his family and keep a roof overhead.

Sylvester Lanon Brown wasn't born into ease — nobody Black in Mississippi was back then. He was born into labor, into a world that measured a man's worth by how much he could lift, how much he could endure, and how little he complained about it. He was a man whose hands bore the burden of generations — hands that had built other people's houses but never owned one, that had raised crops they didn't get to keep, that had signed pay slips with an "X" where the numbers never seemed to add up right. His fingers never traced words on a page because he hadn't yet learned how to read. Yet somehow, in those same hands, there was pride. The kind that came from doing what needed to be done. From knowing that though the world refused to give him his due, he still gave the world his best.

He didn't have much schooling. Reading and writing weren't things the world thought a Black man needed to know, but he learned what mattered — how to build, how to repair, how to provide. Later in life, he taught himself to read, finally able to trace words with calloused fingers until they made sense. "A man's mind," I can feel him say, "ain't worth nothing if he don't feed it."

When he sat on the porch at night, a fist-full of snuff stuffed in his cheek, he'd rest those heavy hands on his knees and look out across the fields — not with regret, but with quiet knowing. Those hands had done enough to prove he belonged here. They had worked, built, held, protected, and prayed. They had carried more than any one man should, but somehow they never faltered.

And when he reached out to touch your shoulder, it felt like history itself resting there — strong, steady, and unbreakable. He didn't show affection the way Mama did. He wasn't a man of hugs or long talks. But he showed love in the way he made sure we had wood for the fire before winter came, or in how he mended the porch steps so Mama wouldn't trip. His love was practical — measured in full stomachs and steady light. I don't necessarily remember him saying "I love you" out loud; he built it, board by board, meal by meal.

Like every Black man in the South during those years, he carried a quiet fear — not of God, but of what white men might do if he looked too proud or spoke too loud. I saw it in the way he lowered his eyes when we went into town, in how his shoulders tensed when a white man called him "boy." But I also saw pride, not the kind that boasts, but the kind that refuses to break. He walked with dignity even when the world tried to strip it away.

Diddy believed in work — not because he loved it, but because he knew it was the only way to keep his family fed. He taught me that a job well done was its own reward. His work was as if saying to me: "If you start something you finish it. And you do it right." I learned a lot from Diddy — not from his words, but from his ways. He taught me that strength isn't loud, that manhood isn't cruelty, and that silence doesn't always mean weakness. He taught me that love doesn't need to be shouted to be real.

I don't remember him talking much about dreams, but I think he had them — quiet ones. Maybe he dreamed of owning land one day, of not answering to anyone but himself. Maybe he dreamed of seeing his children live lives that stretched farther than those cotton fields. He never said it, but sometimes I caught him staring out past the trees at sunset, eyes far away, like he could see something better on the horizon.

I must have been about three years old the first time I remember riding out to the fields with Diddy and Mama. I remember the sound before I remember the sight — the slow, steady creak of the wagon wheels turning against the dirt road, the harness jingling as the old mule pulled us through the morning mist. The air was heavy with dew and the smell of turned earth — damp, rich, and alive. Even then, I knew we were moving toward work.

Diddy sat up front, reins in hand, his broad shoulders hunched forward against the rising sun. I remember staring at his hands, gripping those leather straps, knuckles dark and cracked. They looked too big for the reins, too big for the small space they had in the world. Every now and then, he'd click his tongue to the mule, and the animal would grunt, dust rising in soft red clay clouds behind us. Mama sat beside him, her skirt gathered in her lap, her hair tied back with a faded scarf. She looked ahead, quiet, as though the day's labor was already heavy on her mind.

The fields stretched out before us like forever — endless rows of green and brown, cotton plants bowing low under the weight of the South. The sun came up slow, burning off the fog, painting everything gold for just a moment before the heat took over. That was Mississippi: delightful, then devastating.

When the wagon stopped, Diddy lifted me down with those same rough hands — gentle as could be. His palms were calloused, warm, the smell of smoke and sweat clinging to them. He set me in a patch of shade beneath a pecan tree and handed me a piece of cornbread wrapped in a rag. "Stay put," he said softly. Then he and Mama went to work.

I watched them all day. Mama's back bent low, her skirt brushing the dirt as she picked row after row, her hands moving fast but careful, like she'd done it all her life. Diddy worked beside her, his body steady and strong, the muscles in his arms shining with sweat. Sometimes they didn't speak for hours — just moved in rhythm, like a song without words.

The sounds of that day are still in my ears: the rustle of cotton, the creak of the wagon, the hum of cicadas, the wind sighing through the trees. Every so often, Diddy would straighten up, wipe his brow, and look toward me — just to make sure I was still there. And I'd wave, my little hand trying to match the size of his.

When the sun dipped low and the air turned cool, they loaded the cotton, their shadows stretching long behind them. Diddy's hands, those mighty hands, lifted me back onto the wagon like I weighed nothing at all. Mama handed me a piece of cold biscuit and smiled, her face tired but soft.

22

We rode home under a pink sky, over dangerously constructed wooden bridges, the world quiet except for the mule's slow steps and the rhythm of the wheels. I leaned against Diddy's arm and felt the steady beat of his heart beneath the worn fabric of his shirt. I didn't understand then what those days meant — what they cost. But I knew I was safe.

It took me years to understand what I witnessed those days — that long ride on the mule-drawn wagon through the still Mississippi morning. At three years old, I didn't see struggle. I saw routine. I saw love in motion. Now, I understand that what I was watching was survival dressed as simplicity.

Mama and Diddy didn't just work the land — the land worked them. It took pieces of their youth, their health, their peace, and in return gave just enough to keep us alive. But they didn't complain. They never cursed the soil. They treated it like an old friend that didn't always keep its promises but had been there too long to abandon.

That day, I learned that love could look like labor — the kind that leaves your back bent and your hands raw but your heart still full. I saw my father's sweat fall onto the same ground that grew our supper. I saw my mother's fingers, swollen and tired, still reach for mine to hand me bread.

They carried the weight of generations on their shoulders — the burden of poverty, the shadow of racism, the echoes of enslavement, the quiet ache of dreams too dangerous to speak aloud. Yet they kept going, as if the act of continuing itself was a form of praise.

As a child, I didn't know what resilience meant. But I saw it. It was in the rhythm of their movement, in the faith they carried without words, in the small joys they created out of exhaustion. I remember how, even after twelve hours in the field, Mama would hum while cooking supper, and Diddy would sit outside, his hands clasped, eyes lost in the dark — maybe talking to God, maybe to his own weary thoughts.

The weight of their work became the foundation of my life. It taught me that strength isn't loud. That love isn't always soft. It taught me that endurance can be a kind of prayer.

And now, every time I think of that little girl sitting under the pecan tree, watching her parents under the unforgiving Mississippi sun, I realize — that was the day I began to understand what legacy really meant.

They didn't have much to leave behind. No land. No money. No titles. But they left me their will to keep going — and that has carried me farther than I ever thought I'd go.

Now, when I close my eyes, I can still feel the sway of that wagon, smell the earth, hear the hum of the South — and see those two figures in the field, bent but unbroken. Their hands, their sweat, their sacrifice, a foundational chapter in my story of becoming.

Chapter 5 | Ol' Miss

Oxford, Mississippi, in the early 1950s was a place that could steal your breath — both for its beauty and for its brutality. The land itself was alive, rich with red clay that used to stain my bare feet, my soles, and my soul, fields stretching wide beneath skies that always seemed too big for the sorrow they held. Cotton grew tall in the summer sun, its white blooms rippling across the hills like snow, and the air smelled of earth, sweat, and mule leather.

The mornings began with the sound of roosters and the slow creak of wooden screen doors, and by noon, the heat hung so heavy you could taste it. Cicadas sang their long, droning songs, and the air shimmered above the dirt roads. Pine trees lined the edges of the fields, whispering secrets whenever the wind passed through them. Everything about Oxford was both humble and holy — a place where beauty and struggle lived side by side.

But beneath that postcard peace was a current of fear and division. The 1950s in Mississippi were Jim Crow years. Those were the years when every person knew their place or was made to. There were two Oxfords then: one for white folks and one for us. Downtown had its shops, its courthouse square, its drugstores with polished counters and "Whites Only" signs. We could walk through, but we couldn't stay long. Colored folks had to use the back doors or the side windows.

Schools were separate, churches were separate, even the cemeteries were divided by race. In the courthouse, the water fountains told you who you were before anyone said a word — "White" and "Colored," carved in metal like commandments. We didn't question it aloud, but it seemed so normal to me that I couldn't fully feel the wrongness, that it certainly was, deep in my bones. You could be polite, hardworking, respectful, and still I'd be called "girl" or my brothers and father called "boy" by a man half his age if his skin was white. That was the law of the land — not written in the Bible but written into everything else.

Most Black families lived on the edges of town, in wooden houses that leaned a little after every storm. Some worked as maids, cooks, or field hands. Others, like my father and mother sharecropped, trading their labor for a portion of the harvest — though most times, the math never seemed to add up in their favor. The landowners kept the books, and somehow the debt always grew no matter how hard folks worked.

But still, life went on. On Saturdays, the juke joints came alive on the outskirts of town. You could hear blues drifting through the night air — muddy and sweet, like the Delta itself. Men played dominoes on makeshift tables, women fried catfish in cast iron skillets, and laughter rose up like a hymn that refused to die. The smell of fried cornmeal, tobacco, and magnolia blossoms filled the air.

Sundays were different. The same people who had danced on Saturday dressed in their best and walked down red-dirt paths to church. The sound of tambourines, foot-stomps, and harmony carried through the fields. Church was more than worship — it was release, it was resistance, it was where people remembered that even if the world outside refused to see their worth, God still did. I loved it when my father, whom I called "Diddy," took me with him to church. Mama didn't much like going. The energy and atmosphere have given me a life-long calling towards God.

Oxford was also the kind of place where news traveled faster than wind. Everyone knew everybody. A baby born, a man fired, a girl gone north — it all made its way from porch to porch, whispered over wash lines and store counters. The white folks' world might have had politics, but the Black folks' world had its own kind of governance — built on respect, reputation, and resilience.

By 1955, when I was still a little girl, the winds of change were starting to stir, though we didn't yet know their names — Brown v. Board of Education, Rosa Parks, Montgomery. But even before those stories reached us, we could feel something rising in our spirits, a quiet knowing that the world wouldn't stay the same forever.

Still, in Oxford, Mississippi, in those years, the land remained red, the cotton white, and the lines between us black, white and gray, but still clear as ever. But even then, under the shadow of segregation, love grew. Families laughed. Children dreamed. And every morning, the sun rose over those Mississippi hills as if to remind us — no matter what laws men wrote, God was still in charge of the dawn.

Looking back now, I realize Oxford taught me two kinds of lessons — the ones you could see and the ones you could feel. The land taught me beauty: the sway of the pines, the hum of summer heat, the music that rose from front porches and cotton rows. But the world around me taught me caution. Every "Whites Only" sign, every stare that lingered too long, every whispered warning from Mama carved something deep inside me — not bitterness, but awareness.

As a child, I didn't understand that I was growing up in a system built to keep me small. But Mama did. Grandma did. Diddy did, and got up every day and worked, not necessarily "in spite of," rather "because of" the fact he had a family to feed. My parents had already learned how to walk the fine line between survival and dignity. They knew how to smile when it was required and how to stay silent when speaking could cost too much.

And yet, within all that restriction, they still managed to live full lives — to sing, to cook, to love, to teach. Oh, what a beautiful singing voice Mama had. That was their quiet rebellion. They didn't let Jim Crow define their joy. They made homes that felt like freedom, even when the world outside said they weren't free at all.

Those early years in Oxford shaped me in ways I'm still uncovering. They gave me a faith that could weather anything, a resilience born from the women before me, and a voice I didn't always use, but always carried.

I learned that strength isn't about shouting louder than the world — it's about standing firm when the world tries to silence you. Oxford showed me that even in the shadow of injustice, grace can still take root. And from that red Mississippi soil, I learned the greatest truth of all: that love — real, enduring love — can bloom anywhere, even in the hardest ground. Even in the infertile soil of injustice. Even in the barren fields of cruelty. Love blooms where there is love, family, joy, peace, sacrifice, where it is watered with tears, and smiles give it light.

Chapter 6 |
Heirloom

My father's road to meeting my mother wasn't a straight one. Before her, there was another life — a first wife, a small house, and two children he loved but rarely spoke of. Their names floated through our home like quiet ghosts, mentioned only in passing and always softened by time. I didn't grow up close to them; life and distance made sure of that. But their story was woven into ours long before I was born.

From what I was told, his first marriage began the way many did back then — young hearts, big dreams, and the hope that hard work could keep love alive. But life in Mississippi wasn't kind to families, especially Black ones trying to hold on to something of their own. The weight of poverty, the strain of long hours in the fields, and the unspoken pressure of survival wore people thin. And somewhere along the line, that woman — his first wife — reached her breaking point.

The story goes that one hot afternoon, she loaded their two small children into the backseat of an old car and drove out to the edge of town — a lonely stretch of land where the road gave way to the fields. She left them there, those babies, with no food, no water, and no promise that she'd return. Then she drove away — north to Michigan, chasing a new life, or maybe just running from the old one.

My father found out when someone from town came running to tell him. I can only imagine the panic in his chest as he dropped everything and ran. I see him now in my mind — a younger version of the man I knew — his work boots pounding the dirt, calling out their names until his voice went hoarse. And then, finding them there, those two frightened little faces looking up at him with tears and dust on their cheeks.

He never really talked about what that moment did to him, but I saw traces of it in his eyes — the quiet sadness, the protectiveness, the way he held his children and grandchildren close even years later. He took them home, washed their faces, and quietly vowed to raise them himself. From that day forward, with the help of a village of Oxford Mississippians he became both father and mother, doing whatever it took to keep them safe and fed, and to ensure they knew what love felt like.

It couldn't have been easy. There was no daycare, no financial assistance, no government program waiting to step in. Just a man, his faith, and his will to keep going. My aunt — his sister Sarah — helped when she could, watching the children while Diddy worked the fields or took odd jobs. Together, they did what family has always done in our line — they made a way out of no way. Because there was no way he was going to discard his babies.

Perhaps that experience shaped him more than anything else. It made him cautious, made him slow to trust, made his heart both tender and guarded. By the time he met my mother years later, he was a different man — older, quieter, and determined never to lose the people he loved again. Diddy carried that first heartbreak with him like a scar — invisible, but always there. And though I never knew the woman who left or the reasons she carried in her heart, I do know this: her leaving carved something in my father that he turned into strength.

As the children entered adulthood and decided what they wanted for their lives, my father tarried on with the routine of work and church. His faith in God never wavered through any struggle he endured. And maybe that's why, when he built a new family with my mother, he built it steady. No grand promises, no fairytales — just the daily act of showing up, providing, protecting, enduring. He had already seen what it looked like when love gave out. So this time, he made sure it lasted until death parted them.

It took me years to understand that a man's silence can be a kind of grief. When I was a child, I used to wonder why Diddy never talked much about his past — about the woman who left or the children he raised before me. He'd just look away when their names came up, his jaw tightening the way it did when he was fighting tears he'd never let fall.

Now, I know that some stories aren't told because they hurt too much to hold in the open air. Some pain becomes part of your bones — you carry it, you build around it, and you keep on living. That's what he did. What I have had to do.

His heartbreak became a lesson — one I didn't truly understand until I became a wife myself. They say a woman often marries a reflection of her father, and in my case, that might be true. The man I have loved and lived beside for nearly sixty years carries a story that, in some quiet way, mirrors my father's own. Both men were shaped by loss — not the loud kind that comes with death, but the quiet kind that lingers in absence.

My father's pain began in a Mississippi field, standing beneath a sky too wide to hold his grief, clutching the small hands of two children who had just been left behind. My husband's sorrow came years later, in a different season, when he made the hardest choice a man can make — to walk away from four of his own. Different reasons. Different roads. But the same ache threaded through both of them — that hollow, unspoken wound of separation.

Through my husband, I've seen that same shadow cross a man's face — the mixture of pride and regret, of strength carrying the weight of what could not be mended. There are moments when I look at him and see a trace of my father: that same silence that holds a thousand untold apologies, that same determination to rebuild what life once broke.

It's strange how love travels through generations — how pain can be passed down not as bitterness, but as wisdom. My father rebuilt his life with my mother, just as my husband and I built ours from the ashes of what came before. In each of our homes, there was an unspoken vow: that no one under this roof would ever feel the sting of abandonment again. Sadly, it was a vow that wasn't always kept.

I've seen what brokenness can do to a man — how it hardens him or humbles him. This is the inheritance I have received. From my father, I inherited endurance — the ability to keep moving even when the world feels heavy. From my husband, I inherited grace — the quiet kind that comes from learning to love someone through their scars, their flaws, their selfishness, not around them. And from both, I inherited an understanding that healing isn't a single moment. It's a lifetime of small choices to keep showing up.

There's a certain kind of beauty in watching a man who once knew loss learn how to love again — not with the reckless passion of youth, but with the deliberate tenderness of someone who understands what's at stake. That's the kind of love I've known for most of my life. The kind that endures. The kind that forgives. The kind that stays.

And in that staying, I learned something my father never said but always lived: that love, real love, doesn't erase pain — it redeems it. But I've also seen what redemption can do — how it softens the edges, how it turns regret into resolve. Both my father and my husband taught me that love is not measured by perfection, but by persistence. They didn't run from their pain; they built something from it.

And in this way, we became builders of belonging. Every meal cooked, every laugh shared, every argument forgiven — it was all part of the rebuilding, the daily choosing to stay. Because both of the men who shaped my life had known what it felt like to be hurt. Both have weaponized their pain to inadvertently hurt others. Both of them have known what it felt like to be left. And both of them — in their own time and their own way — made sure I never had to know that same kind of loneliness.

I used to think inheritance was about what people left behind — land, money, or keepsakes wrapped in old newspaper. But as I've grown older, I've learned that the truest inheritance is what people leave *within* you.

So, when I look at my family now — at my children, my grandchildren, and the life we've built brick by brick — I see the legacy of two men who taught me how to turn heartbreak into hope. Their stories didn't end with abandonment; they ended with belonging.

That is the inheritance I carry. Not just the memory of loss, of pain, betrayal, but the miracle of what survived it.

Chapter 7 | Chosen

Diddy's marriage to Mama wasn't born out of love — at least, not the kind you read about in books, passionate greeting cards, or see in the movies. It was arranged, plain and simple.

The way I understand the story of their union was something like this: One afternoon, my grandfather looked at my father and said, "You see my daughter there? She's a good woman. You're a good man. It's time for her to have someone to take care of her. You'll marry her." And that was that. No proposal, no courting, no long letters exchanged between sweethearts — just an understanding sealed by the authority of elders and the customs of the time.

Diddy, about thirty-eight or forty at the time, agreed without hesitation. In those days, a man didn't question an offer like that — especially not from someone he respected. And Mama? Well, I guess she didn't have much of a say. She was twenty-six then — old enough to be considered past her prime for marriage in the eyes of many, but still young enough to be told what to do. That was the world she lived in. Back then, love wasn't a prerequisite for marriage. Stability was. Respect was. Survival was.

So they married not because they were in love, but because life demanded partnership more than passion. It was a practical arrangement — two people bound by duty, tradition, and a shared will to make things work.

For women like my mother, obedience wasn't a virtue — it was a necessity. In her time, saying *yes* wasn't about agreement; it was about survival. A woman's worth was measured by how well she could keep a home, how quietly she could swallow disappointment, and how faithfully she could stand beside a man who might not see her heart, but needed her hands.

Mama's generation was taught that love was something you grew into, not something you chose. You didn't question your place in the world because the world didn't leave much room for questions. A good woman stayed. A good wife obeyed. A good mother endured.

And endure, she did.

She endured through the heat of Mississippi summers, through winters where the wood stove burned low, through years of scarcity and silence. Her kind of strength didn't look heroic — it looked ordinary. But that quiet obedience carried the weight of generations.

Still, obedience came with a cost — one I saw even before I could name it. It dimmed something in her. Not her light entirely, but the freedom to shine how she wanted. I think about that sometimes — how many dreams were folded neatly away inside her apron pockets, how many thoughts she swallowed just to keep peace.

But I also see the gift hidden inside her restraint. Her silence made me hungry for words. Her submission made me crave choice. Her endurance taught me not just how to survive, but how to demand something more from life — something that looked like joy, even if only experienced by the children someday.

So she endured and they built a life that was steady if not tender. Mama ran the house like a small kingdom — meals cooked from scratch, laundry washed by hand, floors swept until they shined. Diddy worked long hours and kept order with a firm voice and, when needed, a heavy hand. They paid their bills, raised their children, and showed up for one another in the quiet, consistent way that counted back then.

I never saw them kiss. I never heard "I love you." Their affection lived in unspoken gestures — in a plate of food set aside, in a shirt ironed just right, in the way Mama would pull his chair out at supper or the way Diddy made sure her firewood was always stacked high for winter. Their love was not poetic, but it was practical. It wasn't the kind that made you swoon — it was the kind that kept you fed, clothed, and safe.

Still, as I grew older, I could tell that something softer had formed between them — not romance, exactly, but a mutual respect, maybe even quiet admiration. They never said it aloud, but sometimes love doesn't need words. It just shows up in the way two people keep choosing to stay, even when life gives them reasons to walk away.

But I also knew, deep down, that I wanted something different. I admired their endurance but longed for something more than arrangement — I wanted affection, laughter, choice. Maybe that's why I promised myself that when my time came, nobody — not Diddy, not society, not even tradition — was going to pick a husband for me.

And Lord knows, Diddy tried.

He once brought home a man named Spencer — one of his friends from an adult literacy class. Diddy saw in him what he thought mattered: a job, a willingness to learn, and good manners. He figured that was enough for happiness. But I knew better. Spencer was kind but not for me — a man of my father's choosing, not my heart's. I remember Diddy saying, "He's steady, Janice. He'll take care of you." His brother was cute, but Spencer was not. Not in the least bit. But ugly or not, I didn't like the idea of someone choosing for me.

44

I wanted something more for my life. I wanted to be *somebody*. Not just somebody's wife or somebody's daughter — just somebody. Education was my way out, my way up, and my way forward. By the time I got to college, I wasn't just learning from books — I was learning how to build a life that belonged to me.

Southern Illinois University was a world away from my beginnings in Oxford, Mississippi. The air smelled different — less of soil and woodsmoke, more of possibility. I worked in the campus cafeteria to pay my way, serving students who, like me, were trying to earn both an education and a little dignity. The rhythm of that place was familiar: trays clattering, laughter echoing across linoleum floors, the hum of vending machines that never quite worked right.

And then one day, he walked in.

I remember it as clearly as if it were yesterday. Tall, confident, carrying himself with that quiet kind of ease that draws attention without demanding it. He came through my line, paid for his lunch, and just as I was about to hand him his change, he slapped something on the counter — two tickets. "Here," he said, his voice deep but playful. "These are tickets to a concert. Be ready at eight."

I froze for a second, staring at those tickets like they were golden keys. A concert? I had never been to one in my life — let alone a *symphony orchestra*. I'd grown up listening to gospel and blues, to the hum of the fields and the clatter of dishes. Violins and tuxedos weren't part of my world. And yet, something in me stirred.

It wasn't just curiosity. It was the feeling of being *seen.* Chosen.

But more than that — it was the feeling of *choosing back.* For the first time, I wasn't waiting for someone to tell me what I should do, who I should be, or whom I should love. I was standing on my own two feet, in my own story, ready to decide for myself.

I looked up at him — this man whose name I didn't even know yet — and before reason could catch up to courage, I smiled and said, "Yes."

He grinned, picked up his tray, and started to walk away. But just before he disappeared into the noise of the cafeteria, he turned back and asked, "Hey… just how old are you?"

I felt that mischievous spark rise in me — that little bit of boldness I had inherited from all the women before me who had quietly wished for more. I tilted my head, gave him my best shy, flirtatious grin, and said, "Old enough."

His name was Fred — Frederick Leon Slack, Sr. That day — Friday, January 17, 1969 — became the first page of a new chapter in my life.

I was eighteen years old — still balancing on the edge between girlhood and womanhood, between the lessons I had been taught and the life I was determined to create. He was thirty-one, already a man with stories of his own, carrying the weight of experience I hadn't yet known. But that didn't scare me. Because for the first time, I wasn't following a path that someone else had chosen. I was choosing my own.

And I didn't know where it would lead, but I knew this much: I was ready — ready for love, ready for life, ready to finally become the woman I had always imagined I could be.

I think Mama understood that, even if she never explicitly said it. She had lived the life chosen for her. She wanted more for me, even if she couldn't quite name it. And maybe that's the quiet gift she left me — the courage to want love on my own terms. Because if my parents' marriage taught me anything, it's that endurance can hold a family together — but only love, the kind that's freely given, can make it flourish.

Even as I was choosing for myself, I could not choose the world in which I lived. The world had changed by the time I came of age, but not enough. Expectations still clung to women like a second skin — be quiet, be pretty, be grateful for what you're given. And still, I felt Mama whispering in my ear: *Don't lose yourself like I did. Don't trade your voice for someone else's comfort.*

So I didn't.

It has taken some years, but I learned that obedience without understanding is just fear dressed as faith. I learned that endurance without purpose is just pain mistaken for love.

And though I carry my mother's lessons, I also carry her longing — that silent prayer she never spoke out loud: that one day her daughters and granddaughters would be free enough to love not because they were told to, but because they chose to.

That's a gift I took from her — not obedience, but courage. Not silence, but speech. Not endurance for its own sake, but the strength to create and choose a life on my own terms.

And in that way, I like to think that throughout my life I have honored her — not by living exactly as she did, but by living the life she never had the chance to choose.

Chapter 8 | Black Horse

Mama was jolly when I was small — sunlight wrapped in an apron. She had a song for every moment of the day, like music was stitched into her bones. She'd hum gospel while hanging clothes on the line, her voice rising and falling with the wind as the white sheets swayed like sails against the sky. In the kitchen, she'd laugh while stirring a pot of greens, hips moving with a rhythm older than time, tapping the spoon against the pot like it was a drum. Even her sighs sounded like melody. I didn't say much back then, just watched her in the kitchen, absorbing her ways like osmosis does when raisins swell soaking in water.

Mama was a natural storyteller, too. When the day's work was done and the kerosene lamps flickered low, she became something close to magic. We'd sit cross-legged on the floor, wide-eyed, shadows dancing on the walls, while her voice painted pictures we could almost see. She didn't need books or paper; her stories lived in her — inherited from her mother and her mother's mother before her, carried through time like sacred fire.

We didn't have a television back then, just Mama's imagination — and that was plenty. She could make ghosts walk and animals talk, make the wind whisper secrets to the trees, and make us believe every word. Sometimes she'd scare the life out of us with her ghost stories, her voice dropping low and slow, her eyes wide and wild. Then, right when we were leaning in close, she'd jump up and grab us, laughing so hard she could barely breathe. We'd scream and tumble over one another, hearts pounding, half terrified and half delighted. That was our entertainment, our joy, our world.

But my favorite was the story of the big black horse.

Mama had a way of telling it like she'd lived it herself. She'd settle into her chair, light glinting off her eyes, cigarette in the corner of her lip, and begin in that soft, powerful, knowing voice of hers.

"There was once a black horse in a pasture," she'd say, letting the words roll out slow. "The most beautiful horse you ever did see — strong, shining, standing tall in the sunlight."

Her tone would shift, low and serious. "Then some kids came by and started teasing that horse — calling him names, throwing rocks at him, laughing. The horse didn't move. He just stood there, quiet and still. They hit him again and again, in the face, on the side. But he didn't kick, didn't run, didn't flinch."

Mama would pause then, letting the silence hang heavy like the moment before a storm. "Finally," she'd say, her voice deepening, "when they'd worn themselves out, that horse lifted his head and said…" — and here she'd lower her tone to a whisper so soft we had to lean in close — "'Are you through? Have you done all you can do?'"

Then she'd grin, eyes twinkling, and roar in a voice that made us all jump — "'Because now,' said the horse, 'it's my turn!'"

We'd shriek, clutching one another, and she'd laugh until her shoulders shook. Every time she told it, it felt brand new.

I didn't understand the meaning when I was little. To me, it was just another of Mama's stories — funny, scary, silly, and full of life. But as I got older, I realized it wasn't just a story. It was a sermon wrapped in laughter.

That tale of the black horse was about strength that doesn't need to prove itself. About endurance that doesn't bend under mockery or cruelty. About the power of patience — waiting until the right time to rise. Mama had lived that story long before she ever told it. She was the black horse — calm through storms, silent through struggle, standing strong through life's blows until it was her turn.

That was how Mama taught. She didn't lecture or scold. She taught through stories that stayed with you, sinking deep into your bones. Her lessons arrived like lullabies — soft enough to comfort, strong enough to last a lifetime.

Unlike Diddy, Mama never preached from a pulpit, but she delivered sermons all the same. Her gospel wasn't written in any book — it lived in her laughter, her labor, and her love. She didn't quote scripture; she *was* scripture in motion. Everything she said carried the weight of the Word, even when it came wrapped in humor or a ghost story.

To the outside world, Mama was just a woman raising children in a small Mississippi town. But to us, she was something larger — a teacher, a prophet, a living reminder that joy and struggle could share the same breath. She could make faith feel like a song and strength feel like a story.

Those evenings by the wood burning stove were more than entertainment — they were our education. She taught us about patience through the story of that black horse, about forgiveness through tales of trickster animals who learned better, and about courage through the women in her stories who faced storms and still managed to sing.

We didn't realize she was preparing us for the world outside our door — a world that didn't always listen to women like her, a world that tried to convince you to be small. But Mama's gospel wouldn't allow that. She taught us that being small was never an option. This is why her reassuring voice had me loving my dark brown skin, and had me believing that I was tall.

Her lessons were simple, but they stayed with me: If you fall, get up. If you're scared, sing louder. If the world throws stones, stand still until it's your turn.

As I got older and began raising children of my own, I found her words echoing in my mind, uninvited but welcome — soft as a hymn, firm as truth. I caught myself telling stories the same way she did, letting laughter soften the lesson. That's the gospel according to Mama. Not one written in chapters and verses, but in lived moments — a life that showed me God could speak through ordinary people, through the rhythm of washing clothes, through the melody of a mother's hum, through a story told by the light of a flickering fireplace.

And even now, when I feel lost, I hear her voice again, rising up from memory like a familiar hymn — gentle, steady, unbroken — whispering through memory:

"Are you through? Have you done all you can do? Because now, it's my turn."

Chapter 9 | Worry

The old folks had a saying, *"Worry won't change tomorrow, but it sure will ruin today."* I didn't understand that when I was little. Back then, worry felt like breathing. It lived inside me — quiet but constant. I worried about thunderstorms, about Mama getting sick, that cough from her cigarette habit she started when she was just three years old. About Diddy coming home late. Or him not coming home at all. And on one night in early winter of 1955, I worried more than I ever had in my life.

That was the night we left Oxford.

I didn't know all the reasons then — children never do — but I knew something wasn't right. I could hear it in the way Mama and Diddy whispered after dark, their voices tight like pulled thread. I could hear just about everything in that small one room shack. I could see it in the way Diddy's hands shook when he came home from the fields.

We were sharecroppers, like most Black families in Mississippi back then. Diddy worked another man's land from sunrise to sunset — planting, picking, and praying that this year's harvest might finally be the one to break even. But the numbers never did add up. The man who owned the land — a white overseer with a slick tongue and a pocketbook full of tricks — always found a way to cheat Diddy out of his share.

That year, Diddy realized it wasn't a mistake. It was a setup. He had been working himself into debt for years, a kind of slavery that didn't wear chains but still bound a man just the same.

I remember the tension in the air those last few weeks — Mama packing quietly, perhaps pretending it was just spring cleaning. Diddy meeting with neighbors after midnight. My siblings, Larry, Homer, John, Linda, and I were told to keep our voices down. Sue was not yet born. There was talk — hushed talk — about men who disappeared for asking too many questions. About folks who tried to leave and didn't make it to the next county line. A man's debts could get him hung as a message to the rest that your life was worth less than the coins you owed a white man.

And then, one night, Mama woke me gently. "Baby," she whispered, "get your shoes. We gotta take what we can and leave."

I could hear the crickets outside, the wind rustling through the trees, the faint creak of wagon wheels in the distance. Larry was already up, moving fast but uncharacteristically silent. Mama's hands shook as she buttoned my coat, but her voice was steady. "We're going for a ride," she said. "Stay quiet, and don't look back."

Before we left, I did something small — something that only makes sense to a child. I took my favorite dolls, kissed them goodbye and hid them under some debris on the side of the house. I didn't know Mama would've let me take her. I thought we were coming back. I thought I'd see her again. I thought we'd make our way back home.

We never did.

The car came just after midnight — in it was Aunt Gertrude in an old car that rattled and coughed with every turn. We piled in, bodies pressed together, hearts pounding. The headlights stayed dim, and the driver — a family friend from the church — took the back roads that wound through pine trees and red clay. Every sound made us jump. Every passing light felt like danger.

We reached the bus station before dawn, the air cold and damp with fog. Diddy carried our one suitcase; Mama held a paper bag full of food. We boarded the bus to East St. Louis, Illinois — a place that might as well have been another world.

The driver was a white man with a cruel smirk and a voice that cut like gravel. "Back of the bus, Boy" he barked, before we even found our seats. I froze. My feet wouldn't move, and my throat went dry. I didn't dare speak or breathe too loud. I was too afraid to even ask to use the bathroom during that long ride north. I just sat there, still and small, watching the road disappear behind us.

Mama reached over and took my hand. Her palm was warm, her thumb rubbing circles against my skin. "Don't you worry, baby," she whispered. "We're going someplace better."

I didn't know what "better" meant. I only knew what was. I only knew we were a family, that I was safe and deeply cared for. I didn't know what "better" was. I didn't know if "better" was possible, let alone necessary. I only knew it meant leaving everything I had ever known — the house, the field, the pecan tree, the doll I had hidden beneath the debris on the side of the house. But I held onto her words the whole ride, and I still do.

We arrived in East St. Louis before sunrise, in the early winter of 1955. The city didn't look anything like the Mississippi I'd known — no cotton fields, no tree lines bending in the wind, no dirt roads curling past the horizon. Instead, there were buildings that seemed to touch the sky, streets that smelled like metal and smoke, and people moving fast, faces set hard with purpose.

The air was heavy — not with humidity like back home, but with something invisible and loud: industry. You could hear it in the hum of the trains, the clang of the steel mills, the shouts of men hauling crates down by the river. I remember pressing my forehead to the bus window, watching the sunrise reflect off the Mississippi River, thinking it looked like the same water — but a different world.

Diddy said the North was freedom, but it didn't feel free right away. Freedom, I would learn, had layers. It could be cold and strange and hard to navigate, especially for folks who arrived with nothing but courage and calloused hands.

We stayed first with Mama's sisters, Aunt Pearl and Aunt Velma, women who knew how to bicker, fuss, cuss, and fight one another. There in a house that had us in cramped quarters where the floors creaked and the walls smelled faintly of fried onions and kerosene. There were trains running close enough that the walls shook every few hours, and each time, Mama would look up from whatever she was doing and whisper, "Don't worry, baby. That's just the sound of the city."

For a long time, I didn't sleep well. Every night, I dreamed of Oxford — of red dirt, of pecan trees, of the dolls I had hidden on the side of that Mississippi shack. Sometimes I wondered if she was still there, waiting for me, or if someone had found her and thrown her away. That little doll became the piece of home I couldn't go back for — a symbol of everything we left behind in the dark.

But little by little, we learned how to start again. Mama found work cleaning houses, her hands raw from bleach but her spirit still shining. Diddy took a job at the meatpacking plant, coming home late with tired eyes and the smell of iron and sweat clinging to his clothes. They never complained — not out loud. I think they both knew that complaining wouldn't change a thing. They had gambled everything for a chance to live free, and now it was time to make that freedom mean something.

East St. Louis was a city of contradictions — hope and hardship standing side by side. There were churches on every corner, where southern voices rose in northern air, singing the same hymns that carried us through the fields. There were neighbors who looked out for one another, who shared sugar, and lard for fried chicken, cornmeal for cornbread, and stories and survival tips like sacred secrets.

Mama and Diddy became part of a circle of women, men, family and friends that every Sunday after church, gathered in our home for Sunday dinner. There was coffee and pound cake, they were praying for jobs, for healing, for sons who'd gone off to the army and daughters who'd lost their way. They prayed for the ones still back home in the South, in Mississippi. They played card games and danced and laughed with the ones that were there in the North. And sometimes they smoked, drank and distracted themselves from the illusion that they weren't trapped in the same old system in the North they vowed never to return to in the South.

For me, the North was where I learned to dream beyond survival. For the first five years of my life, I had been thought of as someone who wouldn't or couldn't benefit from schooling because my mute-like demeanor at times gave the false impression that I was socially and academically challenged. Thank God my parents were convinced or compelled to enroll me into school. But I don't think they had high expectations. I went to school and met teachers who looked like me — women who wore bright dresses and spoke with authority, who believed that education could change the course of a life. I started to see myself differently — not just as a sharecropper's daughter, but as a girl with a mind full of possibilities. In school I immediately excelled.

Still, worry followed me like a shadow. I worried that the police would stop Diddy on his way home. I worried Mama's hands would crack open from too much scrubbing. I worried about what we'd do if this new life didn't work out. But Mama's voice stayed in my ear, the same words she'd whispered on that midnight road: *"Don't you worry, baby. We're going someplace better."*

Years later, when I looked back on that time, I realized what she meant. "Better" wasn't a place you found. It was something you built — one long day at a time, one prayer at a time, one act of faith after another.

And though we'd left Mississippi far behind, the lessons we carried from that red clay never left us. We had traded fields for factories, cotton for concrete, but our roots — deep, stubborn, unbreakable — stayed the same. We were people who knew how to survive the impossible. People who had followed the North Star — not in the sky, but in our own hearts.

It wasn't until years later that I understood how close we had come to danger — how Mama and Diddy had quietly planned our escape through a network of family and friends just before the "settlement day" for sharecroppers at the end of December. It was a kind of modern Underground Railroad that helped folks like us get north without questions.

The night we left, they traded fear for freedom. They left behind debt and injustice but also roots and history. They carried nothing but courage, five kids, dignity, self-respect, and a hope they couldn't afford to lose.

Sometimes, even now, when I feel worry creeping back into my bones, I remember that night — the whisper of the road, the hum of the bus engine, the steady warmth of Mama's hand. The old folks carry a special wisdom after all. Worry didn't change tomorrow. But faith — quiet, trembling faith — most certainly did.

Chapter 10 | DSS

They say motherhood changes with each child, and now, looking back, I know that's true. Each of my four children came at a different season of my life — each one teaching me something new about love, patience, and the quiet strength it takes to raise a family in a world that doesn't always make room for you.

My first child, my daughter, was born on December 31, 1973 — right at the edge of a new year, a bridge between who I had been and who I was becoming. She taught me what it meant to love without fear. When I held her for the first time, I didn't just see a baby — I saw every prayer I had ever whispered made flesh. She was soft and alert all at once, like she already knew she had work to do in this world. Her birth ushered in a gentleness in me I didn't know existed — a patience that grew out of awe. She taught me how to nurture, how to listen, and how to begin again.

Then came my first son on June 8, 1976, just three days before I walked across that graduation stage with my bachelor's degree in hand. He arrived right in the middle of my ambition — and yet, he reminded me that achievement means nothing without love to come home to.

He had a calm strength even as a baby, and as he grew, I saw so much of his father in him — the quiet determination, the steady spirit, the sense that no matter what the storm brought, he would find a way to stand.

Those two — my first daughter and son — became my reason for everything. They were the "why" behind my every decision. They watched me grade papers late at night, cook dinner after long days, and pray over bills and blessings alike. They saw me tired but never defeated. I wanted them to know that faith and work ethic were not opposites — they were partners.

For years, it was just the four of us — me, their father, and our two growing children — learning how to build a home one day at a time. But then, when I thought my childbearing years had passed, God surprised me again.

On December 20, 1987, I gave birth to my second son. I was older then — steadier, wiser, more grounded in faith. His birth felt different, like a second wind of motherhood. He was my reminder that life always has room for joy — that even when you think you've seen it all, God will send you something new to remind you of His goodness. He had an easy smile, a sweet spirit, and a curiosity that filled the house with laughter. Raising him while guiding teenagers was no easy task, but it made me stretch my heart wider. I became softer again — the kind of softness that only comes with perspective.

And then, on February 24, 1990, came my baby girl — the final piece to the puzzle of my family, the one who completed the circle. Her arrival was like spring after a long winter — unexpected, refreshing, and full of life. By then, I had learned not to rush through the moments. I held her longer, kissed her forehead more often, and memorized the small sounds she made when she slept. She came into a home already built on stories, songs, and faith — a home where her siblings helped raise her, and her laughter reminded us all that joy multiplies when it's shared.

Each child changed me — not just as a mother, but as a woman. Dountonia made me tender. Derrick made me strong. Derrin made me hopeful. Dyanna, named for my grandmother, made me whole.

Motherhood was never without its flaws and failings — but it certainly is a product of purpose. It stretched me in ways nothing else could. It taught me how to pray more than I spoke, how to listen more than I lectured, and how to forgive both myself and others when I fell short. It has taught me to pull in tighter, and also when to let go, let God.

There were hard days — the kind that tests your patience and your peace. Days when money was tight, when tempers were shorter than the hours in the day, when I wondered if I was doing enough. Or if I was doing too much. But then there were moments that made it all worth it — bedtime giggles, homemade birthday cakes, the sound of "Mama!" shouted across a room, proms, graduations, grandchildren.

I raised my children to be kind, to work hard, to respect themselves, and to know whose they are — not just who they are. I told them that the world wouldn't always be fair, but they must always be faithful. That people may not always love them right, but God always will. That no matter how far they go, they come from strong stock — from women and men who survived storms, fled fields, escaped enslavement, built lives from scratch, and stood on faith when nothing else stood with them.

Now, when I look at the four of them — grown, grounded, thriving — I see the living legacy of my prayers. Each one carries a piece of me, and together, with twelve children of their own between them, they tell the story of a woman who gave everything she had and still found more to give. I've asked for nothing in return but have received so much more than I ever imagined possible.

Motherhood didn't just teach me how to raise children — it taught me how to raise *myself.* How to rise when weary. How to love without limits. How to build something that lasts beyond my lifetime. And that, I suppose, is the true balancing act of it all — not keeping everything in place, but keeping love at the center, no matter how many plates you're spinning.

There comes a time in every mother's life when the house grows quiet — not empty, just still. You look around and realize that the toys are gone, the laundry is lighter, and the noise that once filled every corner has been replaced by silence that feels both peaceful and unfamiliar.

That's when you know you've entered a new season of motherhood.

When my children were small, my love was hands-on — the kind you could feel. I braided hair, packed lunches, ironed clothes, and wiped tears. I knew where everyone was at all times, what they ate, who their friends were, and when they were up to something they shouldn't be. Back then, my love was loud — it cooked, it cleaned, it prayed out loud in the next room. But as they grew older, my love had to learn how to *quiet down*. It had learned how to step back, unclench its grip, and trust the seeds I had already sown.

That was hard for me. Very hard. I think it's hard for every mother — learning to let go while still holding on in your heart. There's no manual for that kind of transition. You spend years teaching them how to walk, only to spend the rest of your life watching them walk away — praying they'll always know that they can find their way back home even as they are building theirs.

My children became adults one by one, and with each milestone — the graduations, the weddings, new houses, businesses, the babies of their own — I learned to mother differently. My advice became softer, my prayers stronger. I stopped trying to fix everything and started trusting that God would finish the work I began.

There were moments when they didn't need me the way they used to, and that stung a little. But then I realized — that's what motherhood is supposed to do. You raise them to stand tall enough to reach the world without you holding them up. You raise them to love boldly, to fail gracefully, and to remember who they are even when life tries to make them forget.

Each of my four children carries a different piece of me: One has my determination. Another, my stubborn streak. One inherited my love for writing, and another, my deep love for people. Together, they are the mosaic of my motherhood — each unique yet bound by the same thread of faith and family.

As the years passed and life tested me — illness, loss, and aging — I found that my children began to mother *me*. They called to check in, drove me to appointments, reminded me to rest, and made sure I knew how loved I was. It's a strange thing, being cared for by the ones you used to carry. It humbles you. It heals you. It shows you that all those nights of worry, sacrifice, and prayer were never in vain.

I've learned that the seasons of a mother's love are much like the seasons of life itself. Spring is for nurturing — full of growth and discovery. Summer is for celebration — for watching your children bloom. Autumn is for reflection — when the house quiets and you see the beauty in what's been built. And winter — oh, winter is for gratitude — for watching the harvest of your love play out in the lives of those you raised.

Now, when I see my grown children — building their own families, chasing their own dreams — I no longer worry the way I used to. Well, not as much as I used to. But I've traded worry for wonder. I marvel at who they've become, and I thank God for every season we've shared.

I still pray over them every night, but my prayers sound different now. They're not the frantic kind, full of fear and pleading. They're prayers of praise and peace. *"Thank You, Lord, for keeping them. Thank You for keeping me. Thank You for letting me live long enough to see the fruit of my labor."*

Motherhood never ends — it just evolves. The same arms that once held them now fold in prayer for them. The same voice that once corrected them now speaks blessings over them. And the same heart that once feared letting them go now rejoices in watching them fly.

If I've learned anything through the seasons of motherhood, it's this: Love doesn't weaken with age. It deepens. It ripens. It becomes more forgiving, more patient, more sure of itself. I am proud of the mother I've been — not because I did everything right, but because I loved through every wrong.

And when my time comes, I want you, my children, to remember this truth: Your mother loved you in every season — with hands, with heart, and with a faith that never let go. Thank you Dountonia, Derrick, Derrin, and Dyanna, for choosing me to be your mother. For allowing me to pour love into each of you. For the gift of presence, and the presence of the beautiful. I am proud of who you are becoming. And although my life is yet unfinished, you have certainly made it complete.

Chapter 11 | All Joy

There have only been 165 days of my adult life when I have not carried the title of *wife.* That's less than six months out of a lifetime — less than a blink in the long story of who I've been. And for all the more than twenty thousand days that have followed since May 10, 1969, I have lived as one half of a promise — not always perfect, not always easy, but always blessed.

In that time, I have seen it all: rainbows and butterflies, yes — but also snowstorms that shook the roof, thunder that rattled the walls, and seasons where silence sat heavier than words. I've known laughter so pure it could heal a wound, and tears that came so strong they baptized my soul.

Marriage — real marriage — is a living thing. It is perennial. It breathes, it bends, it breaks, withers, and it blooms again. It teaches you that love isn't always romance; sometimes it's resilience. Sometimes it's staying when it would be easier, and wiser, to leave. Sometimes it's holding your tongue, holding your peace, holding your faith — even when your heart feels heavy.

There were years that felt like spring, when love was effortless and joy spilled over like sunlight through open windows. There were years that felt like winter, cold and quiet, where we had to remember why we started or find a new reason to begin anew. But through it all — every season, every joy, every ache — I learned that love, like faith, grows strongest in the storm.

I have lived through dreams realized and dreams deferred. Through nights when the future looked bright and others when it seemed to vanish altogether. Through the miracle of new life, the heartbreak of loss, the slow ache of aging, and the fierce joy of still being here — together.

And still, through it all, my faith teaches me to *count it all joy.* Not because everything has been easy, but because everything has been *mine* — given, endured, and received with grace. I count it all joy because I have loved deeply, even when it hurt. I count it joy because I have been loved through every season. I count it joy because the storms have not drowned me, and the sunshine has not spoiled me.

My life — every second, every minute, every hour, every year — has been a blessing. Not because it has been perfect, but because it has been *purposeful.*

And when I look back now — over fifty years of vows and valleys, laughter and loss — I can say, without hesitation, that joy was never the absence of struggle. It is the strength of my faith in God that carried me through it.

People often ask me what the secret is — how two people can stay together for so long. I never quite know how to answer, because the truth is, it's not one thing. It's a thousand little things done every day, even when you don't feel like doing them. It's love and labor braided so tightly together you can't tell one from the other.

The measure of a marriage isn't taken on the wedding day, when the world is clapping and the cake is sweet. It's taken in the quiet — in the days when you wake up and choose each other again, even when choosing feels like work.

In the beginning, marriage feels like a song — every note bright, every chord alive. You dance through the melody, convinced it will always sound that way. But time teaches you that every song changes. The rhythm slows, the words deepen, and sometimes you lose the tune altogether. That's when you learn what love really means — when you stop dancing *for* joy and start dancing *through* the hard parts.

Over the years, I learned that love isn't built in the big moments. It's built in the ordinary ones — in the meals cooked and the clothes folded, in the laughter that breaks through after a long argument, in the silent forgiveness that passes between two people who've both said too much.

It's built in the waiting — waiting for the paycheck, waiting for the apology, waiting for the season to pass. It's built in the tending — tending to wounds that don't heal right away, tending to dreams that take longer than expected, tending to the bond that keeps stretching but refuses to break.

There were seasons when I didn't recognize us. When the air between us was thick with words unsaid - or said too harshly, when life felt heavy, when we were more partners than lovers, more roommates than companions. But even then, I never doubted that we were *anchored*. Love, I've learned, doesn't always feel like butterflies — sometimes it feels like roots.

There's a strength that comes from surviving together — from building something that lasts through loss, through joy, through silence, through laughter. It's the strength of two people who know each other's wounds and still choose to stay close.

Marriage taught me that forgiveness isn't a one-time act; it's a lifelong practice. You forgive the little things and the big things — sometimes the same things, again and again. You learn that love is not about keeping score but about keeping faith. And faith — that's the real glue. Faith in God, faith in each other, faith in family, in the belief that the story isn't over even when the pages get messy.

There were days when I wanted to walk away. Days when the silence was louder than any shouting could be. But then, I'd remember the promises we made — not just to each other, but to the God who joined us.

Now, after nearly six decades, I can tell you this: The measure of a marriage isn't how easy it's been — it's how faithfully you've endured. It's not the flowers or the anniversaries, but the storms you survived and the prayers you whispered when no one was listening.

If I could go back and tell that young bride anything, standing there on May 10, 1969, nervous and hopeful, 1,697 days away from becoming a mother, I'd tell her this: *You won't always get it right. But you'll always get through it. And in the end, love will be the story that survives you both.*

Because when all is said and done, the measure of a marriage isn't in the years you've spent together. Time does not heal all wounds. It's in the life you've built between those years, the maturation process of learning who you are, entering into this union an adult but not yet grown. It is love— the quiet, steady, enduring kind of love that still says "yes" after all this time.

Chapter 12 | The Dew

I was born in a storm, one the fiercest on record, yet it wasn't even the worst storm I've had to face in my life. Because the hardest storm I ever faced wasn't a blizzard or a flood. It was the day my Mama died. I actually saw her spirit leave her body and ascend as we pushed her onto the hospital elevator. It was 1980.

She wasn't yet even sixty years old — too young, too full of life, too much laughter left to give. Her hands, once strong enough to knead dough and discipline children with a single look, had grown frail. Her voice, once powerful enough to hush a room or lift a hymn, had gone soft. I think it was the cigarettes that took her — slow and cruel, like a thief stealing air one breath at a time.

She started smoking as a little girl, sitting on her daddy's lap. Green Liggins would light one and let her take a puff, thinking it was harmless fun. He didn't know he was planting something that would one day take root in her lungs, that would steal her breath and shorten her years.

When Mama died, I was just approaching thirty. My babies were still small, tugging at my dress, asking questions I didn't have answers for. "Why grandma in that white bed?" the innocent query of my baby boy wanting her to awaken and pour cereal in his bowl again. To hug him again. And all I could think was how unfair it was — that they'd never really *know* her. Not the way I did. Not the way I needed them to.

They'd never really had gotten the chance to feel her laughter shaking through the walls or smell her cooking filling every corner of a house until it felt alive. They'd never sit cross-legged at her feet, listening to her stories — those long, winding tales that could make you cry one minute and laugh the next.

I wanted them to know *her* — her voice, her warmth, her presence — because Mama had a way of making ordinary days feel sacred. And suddenly, all of that was gone. Grief doesn't come in one wave; it comes in ripples — quiet, sneaky ripples that find you over and over again. It doesn't knock. It just shows up.

I remember one day, months after she passed, I was folding laundry. Something simple. Something I'd done a thousand times. And out of nowhere, I smelled her. Not perfume, not smoke — just *her*. That warm, familiar scent that used to fill every room she walked into. It hit me so hard I had to sit down on the edge of the bed. I closed my eyes, and for a moment, I could almost hear her humming. It was like she was standing right beside me — not gone, just changed.

That's when I realized that love doesn't die. It just transforms. It moves from hands to heart, from presence to memory, from voice to echo. If you stay still enough — if you get quiet enough — you can still feel it.

Sometimes, when the wind moves through the trees just right, I swear I can hear her laughter again. When I hum to myself while cooking or tell my grandchildren a story that makes them jump, I know that's her, too. She's not gone. She's woven into me. Into my children. Into everything I touch.

Mama never got to meet all her grandchildren. But I believe she watches over them. Sometimes, when one of my children or grandchildren does something wise beyond their years, that may be *Mama talking through them.*

I think we carry our mothers not in our memories, but in our movements. Every good meal I've ever cooked came from her teaching. Every hard choice I've made came from her strength. Every time I opened my arms when I wanted to close them — that was her too.

It's a strange feeling to realize you've lived more years than the woman who gave you life. There's joy in it, yes — but also a kind of sadness that never goes away. I often think, *Mama, if you could see me now...*

You'd see me cooking your recipes, telling your stories, raising my children with the same mix of love and discipline you gave me. You'd see me laugh the way you used to, head thrown back, eyes closed, unbothered by what anyone thinks. You'd see me finally at peace with who I am.

And I think you'd be proud.

Losing Mama taught me that death doesn't end a relationship — it simply shifts it. She went from being the one who comforted me, to being the one who watches over me. And even though her voice no longer fills my ears, her spirit fills my soul.

That storm broke me for a time, but it also revealed something I didn't understand until years later: Some storms come to destroy. But others come to reveal what's unshakable. And my love for Mama — that's the part that no storm could ever take.

There are some memories that never fade — they don't live in pictures or words, but in the air. For me, Mama lives in the smell of her house.

Even now, all these years later, I can close my eyes and be right back there — that little wooden house with the creaky screen door and the worn rug by the front steps. The moment you walked in, the air felt different — thicker, warmer, like it had a heartbeat of its own.

It smelled like Sunday dinner and Pine-Sol, like cornbread cooling on the counter and clothes drying near the stove. It smelled like laughter and hard work, like prayers whispered over biscuit dough and tears wiped with aprons.

Mama's house always had a rhythm — pots clanging, gospel music humming low from the radio, the hiss of something frying in the pan. Every smell told a story. Every scent carried her spirit.

After she passed, I tried to recreate it. I'd cook her recipes, even scrub the floors with the same cleaner, hoping that somehow the air would feel the same — that she'd walk through the door again, humming, smiling, fussing about something small. But it never quite worked. The secret ingredient was her.

Still, every now and then, the air finds me. I'll be in my own kitchen, stirring greens or folding clothes, and suddenly — there it is. That faint, familiar scent that takes me home in an instant. My throat tightens, my eyes sting, and for a split second, I'm a little girl again, sitting cross-legged on her floor, listening to her stories as the lamp light dances on her face.

That's the power of memory — it sneaks up on you through the smallest things. A smell, a song, a turn of phrase, and suddenly the years collapse into a single heartbeat.

I used to think I lost Mama when she took her last breath. But I know now that she never really left. She just moved into the places where love lingers — in the smell of her house, in the rhythm of my own voice when I pray, in the way my hands fold dough or comfort a crying child.

Her spirit still fills the air, like a smell of the dew after a rain, and every time that scent finds me, I breathe her in again.

Chapter 13 | Cancer

I lost my mother to cancer, a devastating disease that comes and destroys your body and breaks up a home. And for just a moment I thought that my children would feel the pain of losing me the same way I lost Mama. I know this is inevitable to transition from this life, but I wasn't prepared for it to happen sooner than I believed it would or should happen. God holds all the timing, but my life, I feel deeply, is still unfinished.

When I was first diagnosed with cancer, I thought it was a death sentence. I remember the room so vividly — not because of its colors, but because of its *coldness.* The light was too bright, the air too still. The doctor's mouth was moving, but his words felt far away, like water rushing under a bridge. Then came the words that hung in the air like smoke I couldn't breathe through: "It's cancer."

I went home that night and sat in the dark. I didn't cry right away. It was too big to understand, too heavy to hold. When the tears finally came, they came not from fear of dying — but from not being ready to stop *living.*

When the doctor said the word *cancer,* time didn't stop — it just changed. Everything around me blurred —

the ticking clock on the wall, the faint smell of disinfectant, the rustle of his papers. I could hear his voice, but the words slipped past me like water. I remember gripping the edge of the chair to steady myself, not because I thought I might fall — but because, in that moment, I realized life as I knew it had already shifted.

There's a peculiar silence that follows news like that — a silence so loud it echoes inside your chest. You start to remember everything you thought you'd have more time for. You think of your children's faces, your grandbabies' laughter, the dinners you still wanted to cook, the birthdays you still wanted to celebrate.

And then you think of all the times you took the *ordinary* for granted — waking up without pain, brushing your hair, climbing the stairs, singing along with the radio in the car. You realize how fragile "normal" really is.

I went home that night and sat on the edge of the bed for a long time, my husband quiet beside me. There were no words that could make it better. There was only breath — in and out — and prayer, whispered through tears that felt like they'd been waiting their whole lives to fall.

"Lord," I said, "I don't know how to fight this. But if You've brought me to it, I know You'll bring me through it."

And so began the battle within my body.

The treatments came hard and heavy — chemo that burned through my veins, radiation that left my skin tender and raw, fatigue that settled deep into my bones. There were days I couldn't lift my head, days when food lost its taste, days when I didn't recognize the woman staring back at me in the mirror. But even in the mirror, tired and weary, I saw something else beginning to surface — a quiet kind of beauty that had nothing to do with appearance. It was strength. It was grace. It was the woman God had been shaping through every trial that came before.

There were angels around me in that season — not the kind with wings, but the kind who wore scrubs and warm smiles. Nurses who prayed with me before treatment. Friends who cooked meals when I couldn't stand. Family who sat quietly beside me when silence was the only thing that helped.

I remember one night after a particularly rough round, I woke up nauseated and weak, tears streaming down my face. I felt like my body had turned against me. I whispered, "Lord, I can't do this." And in that stillness, I heard it again — that same voice that had guided me through everything else: *"You're not doing this alone. I am with you."*

It wasn't the pain that broke me; it was the grace that humbled me. Because every time I thought I'd reached my end, something — or someone — showed up to carry me a little farther. Like the time I almost drowned.

I remember it so vividly, I must have been no more than three years old when it happened — a small, curious girl playing near the pond that shimmered like a mirror behind our house in Oxford. The grown folks were working the fields that day, and I'd been told a dozen times, *"Don't go near that water."*

But children have a way of testing the edges of the world. So, there I was, probably barefoot in the red Mississippi dirt, stirring up mud pies with a stick, proud of the pretend kitchen I'd made beside that pond. The air was thick with summer — buzzing bumblebees, the smell of damp clay, and the sweet heaviness of honeysuckle drifting from the fence line. Larry was there.

Then, without warning, the ground gave way beneath me. Head over heels — down, down, down into the water. For a moment, everything was quiet. The world above disappeared. No sound. No shouts. Just stillness. The sunlight reached through the water like soft ribbons, and the silt swirled around me like gold dust. It was beautiful — too beautiful for a child to be afraid.

I remember thinking, in that strange calm way only children can think, *"It's peaceful down here. Lord… am I gonna live down here forever?"*

And then — a hand.

A big, strong hand. Rough, warm, certain. It grabbed hold of my arm and pulled me up — through the weight of the water, through the blinding light, into the bright, gasping air.

I coughed and cried, but mostly, I just stared. There was no one there. Larry had run to get Diddy or Mama, and he was too small, just a year older, to help me. My parents were still far in the fields. I looked around for footprints in the mud, for any sign of who had saved me — and there was nothing. Nothing but that steady ripple where I'd fallen, and the soft wind whispering through the trees.

To this day, I don't know whose hand it was. Larry swears it was him. But I know what I *felt*.

That was the first time I ever felt God's hand — real and undeniable. The first time I knew, deep in my small, shivering body, that I was being watched over. That my life — however small, however fragile — was not an accident.

That Hand has been with me through all my sinking moments in my life. And with cancer there were moments of quiet miracles — the day my tests showed signs of progress, the day I could eat again without nausea, the day I saw the first soft fuzz of hair growing back. Each one was a whisper from heaven: *"See? I told you I'd keep you. My Hand is on you."*

When I first got my diagnosis, I thought of my children — their faces, their laughter, their futures — and how much I still wanted to be part of them. I thought of my Mama, how young she was when she left, how her laughter had once filled a house that now only echoed in memory. And I thought, *Lord, please don't let my story end like hers.*

That night, I made a promise: if I woke up the next morning, I'd fight.

And I did.

I prayed, I cried, and I fought — sometimes all in the same hour. Some days I felt like a warrior; other days I felt like a child too tired to lift her head. But every time I wanted to give up, I'd hear Mama's voice — soft but sure — *"Do right, baby. Just do right."* And I knew the right thing wasn't surrender. It was survival.

The treatments were hard. The medicine made me sick. My body, once strong enough to birth babies and bear burdens, grew frail. My hair thinned. My reflection became a stranger. But even then, I remembered where I came from. I was born during the worse storm in history, surely I can weather this one.

And I came from women who endured storms fiercer than this. My grandmother had survived the shadow of slavery. My mother had survived poverty, racism, and heartbreak. And me — I would survive this.

Because endurance was written in my bloodline. Resilience was my inheritance.

I learned to pray differently in those days — not for miracles, but for mercy. Not for a lighter load, but for stronger shoulders. And every morning that I woke up, no matter how weak, I whispered, *"Thank You, Lord, for keeping me."*

Cancer didn't just test my body — it tested my faith, my marriage, my identity. It stripped away everything superficial until all that was left was me — raw, honest, unmasked — and God.

And there, in that sacred space between fear and faith, I learned what true healing feels like. Healing isn't just when the doctor says the cancer is gone. Healing is when you can look at your scars and say, "Thank You." It's when you realize that survival isn't the same as restoration — and yet both are gifts.

I see now that cancer wasn't sent to destroy me — it was sent to *refine* me. To show me what endurance really means. To remind me that God's promises don't crumble under pressure — they reveal their power in the fire.

When people ask me how I made it through, I tell them this: I didn't. God's Hand pulled me through. Every breath, every step, every sunrise since then has been a love note from heaven.

When the sickness passed and the scans came back clean, I didn't shout. I just sat still and wept. Battered, weak, and trembling — but alive.

They called me a *survivor,* and I accepted that title with humility. But over time, I realized survival is more than beating an illness — it's choosing to live *fully* after the battle is over.

I didn't just survive cancer. I survived heartbreak, betrayal, disappointment, and grief. I survived every lie that told me I wasn't enough. I survived the weight of my own worry.

Every wound, every scar, every storm taught me how to bend without breaking — how to let God rebuild me softer, wiser, and stronger than I'd ever been before.

Because cancer didn't take my life. It gave me a new one — one lived in gratitude, one measured not by years but by moments, by breaths, by grace. God, You kept me. Your Hand has pulled me through, keeping me from drowning in despair. Every valley I thought would consume me became a classroom for grace. Even when I thought I was walking alone, You were already walking ahead of me, clearing the path I didn't yet know I'd need.

There were seasons when I didn't see how I would make it. And cancer was no different. When my heart felt too heavy for my chest, when I felt unseen and unwanted in my own home, when words meant to love instead left bruises on my spirit, when friends disappeared, and when family love turned cold — I thought I'd break. But I didn't. I couldn't.

I was born in a snowstorm in Mississippi. There is no way I am going to allow the bitter coldness of cancer defeat me the way all the storms in my life try to.

Chapter 14 | Legacy

They said it never snowed in Mississippi — not like that, not in those days.

That snowstorm Sunday, November 26, 1950 — strange, rare, almost holy — covered everything ugly, every scar, every field that once held our pain. The red dirt turned soft and silent under heaven's blanket. I came into this world under hard skies — a Black girl born in the Deep South, in a time that made you fight for every breath of freedom. But even then, beauty had its way of breaking through. It showed up in Mama's laughter, in Diddy's strength, in the songs we sang to make sense of sorrow.

Life brought me my own storms — storms of heartbreak and betrayal, storms of loss and illness, storms of love that had to learn how to stand again. And yet, through every gust, through every cold and lonely night, God kept me.

I don't see just the pain — I see the pattern. Every trial was a thread, every tear a drop of rain that made something new grow in me. Faith didn't keep me from the storms; it taught me how to dance in the snow. A snowstorm in Mississippi — that's what life has been.

Unexpected. Beautiful. Redeeming. Proof that even in the most unlikely places, God can give birth to wonder.

When I look back over my life, I see a road paved with both beauty and burden — laughter and loss, love and lessons. But above all, I see *grace*. Grace that met me when I was broken. Grace that covered me when I didn't think I'd make it. Grace that walked me through every storm and still whispered, "Keep going."

I have loved and been loved. I have cried and been comforted. I have fallen and been lifted. And through it all, I have seen the hand of God — sometimes gentle, sometimes firm — shaping me into something worthy of the legacy I now leave.

I wasn't perfect, but I was *present*. I wasn't rich in things, but I was wealthy in grace. And I didn't just survive my storms — I found the song inside them.

So, when you read these words, or whisper my name in prayer, don't think of the sorrow. Think of the snow. Think of the stillness after the struggle — when the air is clean, the ground is quiet, and all that's left is love.

Because that's what I leave behind: Not just a brief part of history, but a hymn. Not just a name, but a new beginning. A reminder that even the coldest seasons can become beautiful — when you let the light fall on them just right.

One day I will not be here physically on the earth. And If I could leave behind only one thing, it wouldn't just be money or material things— it would be *meaning.* I want my children, my grandchildren, and their children to know that this life, with all its twists and turns, is worth living when you walk it with purpose and faith.

Lord knows I made mistakes. There were days I was too hard and nights I was too tired. But I loved deeply, even when I didn't have the words to say it right. I prayed over you all more times than you'll ever know — whispered your names into heaven's ear, asking God to make your paths smoother than mine.

Remember this: Faith will keep you when nothing else will. The same God who brought your ancestors out of the cotton fields and into classrooms, out of poverty and into purpose, is the same God who will carry you wherever you're meant to go.

Never forget where you come from. Remember the hands that tilled the land so yours could hold books instead. Remember the women who cooked for others while praying for their own. Remember the men who worked sunup to sundown, not because they had a choice, but because they had a family. Remember their names, their stories, their sacrifices. Because that's how you honor them — by *living fully* and *loving bravely.*

I want you to understand that forgiveness is a kind of freedom. I've learned that carrying bitterness is like drinking poison and expecting someone else to die. Life will hurt you. People will disappoint you. But don't let that harden your heart. Forgive, not because they deserve it, but because *you* deserve peace.

Love, too, will find you in unexpected ways. When it does, hold on — not to the fantasy, but to the friendship. Real love is not perfect; it's patient. It doesn't shout; it shows up. It builds slowly, the way Fred and I rebuild ours after the storms. You don't get to 60 years of marriage without walking through fire — but you come out refined, not burned.

To my daughters: Carry yourselves with grace and confidence. Know that your worth is not in your beauty or your title, but in the way you make others feel seen and loved. The world may try to define you, but remember — you come from a line of women who refused to be boxed in. Stand tall, even when your knees are trembling.

To my sons: Be kind. Be steady. Be men of integrity. Strength isn't in how loud you speak or how much you own — it's in how you treat those with less. Honor the women in your life. Work with your hands but lead with your heart.

And to all my grandchildren — you are the dream made real. You are the answered prayers of generations.

You are the living proof that love endures. Don't rush your life; savor it. Find God early and never let go. Chase purpose, not popularity. Remember that a good name will take you further than gold ever could.

As I near the sunset of my life, I don't fear the night. Because I know the seeds I've planted will keep growing long after I'm gone. And will grow even in the midst of snow. My words, my faith, my love — they'll live in your laughter, your choices, your prayers. That's the beauty of legacy — it doesn't die; it deepens.

If someday you find yourself wondering who you are, open this book and remember: You are the product of love that endured. You are the child of survivors, of dreamers, of believers. You are the living continuation of a story that began long before you and will continue long after.

When my time here is done, don't mourn too long. Celebrate. Cook something I used to make. Sing one of my songs. Tell my stories. Laugh loud. Love hard. And know that I am at peace — because I have seen God's goodness in my lifetime, His Hand pulling up. His grace keeping me grounded. His embrace keeping me warm.

That is my legacy: the light I leave within you. So walk in it. Shine in it. And never forget: You come from love. You are loved. And you will always be my greatest joy.

This is my reflection, my love, my legacy. My Story. My *dream.* **A Life. Complete. Yet unfinished.**

I was born during a snowstorm in Mississippi. I defeated the odds to be here. I was meant to be here. And you are my legacy to ensure I always will.

www.ingramcontent.com/pod-product-compliance
Lightning Source LLC
Chambersburg PA
CBHW021126130626
46554CB00002B/883